How Track Down Dinner

Contents

Do you need a snack?	2
Do not get spotted	4
Be swift	6
Be strong	8
Be clever	10
Never stop	12
Top tips	22

Written by Rob Alcraft

Collins

Do you need a snack?

Be the best hunter you can be! Here are hints and tricks to help you track down lunches, snacks and dinners.

Do not get spotted

Snacks and dinners will **scamper** off if they spot you. Be alert and keep hidden.

Blend in.

Be swift

You must be quick as a flash.
If lunch is near – attack!

A **swift** sprint gets lunch.

Grab a snack and gulp it down.

Do you like munching **crickets**? Then jump for them!

Be strong

Are you extra fit and strong? Go for killer impact.

Power can help get dinner.

Big teeth can snap and crush!

Stun snacks with a swift smack from a flipper.

Be clever

Blend in.

Act like a rock to trick snacks into drifting near you.

Set a trap.

Spin a web that dinner will stick to.

Or just wait!

Pick a spot and grab snacks as they bend down to drink.

Never stop

Never let a good snack slip by.

Get help. Hunting in a **pack** brings down bigger dinners.

Stick at it! This frog has grabbed lunch ... and so can you!

crickets jumping insects
pack a herd
scamper run with quick steps
stun shock
swift quick

Best hunting tricks

Archer fish

Best trick: shoots insects with blobs of spit

Kestrel

Best trick: swift attacks from the air

African hunting dog

Best trick: hunts as a pack to grab bigger dinners

Fearless!

Black mamba

Best trick: injects venom with its fangs

Mantis

Best trick: looks like a twig, but it is a killer

Orca

Best trick: tracks down victims as a pack

Killer swimmers!

Top tips

23

🐾 Review: After reading 🐾

Use your assessment from hearing the children read to choose any words or tricky words that need additional practice.

Read 1: Decoding
- On pages 4 and 5, point to the following words and encourage the children to sound out each letter and blend:

   spotted   snacks   scamper   spot   blend   drift   depths
   - Now challenge them to read pages 4 and 5 fluently. Say: Can you blend the words in your head silently before reading them aloud?
- Read page 8 and focus on the word **impact**. Discuss its meaning in the context of the phrase **killer impact**. (e.g. *effect, result*) Discuss how it shows the drama of the attack because it reminds us of collisions and crashes.
- Bonus content: Challenge the children to read pages 16 and 17 aloud fluently, sounding any words they are uncertain of silently in their heads.

Read 2: Prosody
- Turn to pages 6 and 7 and focus on the punctuation.
   - On page 6, point out the dash and how it tells the reader to pause, and the exclamation mark which shows we must add extra emphasis to the command.
   - On page 7, point to the question mark and the exclamation mark that gives emphasis to the command.
   - Ask the children to read the pages with expression, following the punctuation for extra effect.

Read 3: Comprehension
- Look at the cover photographs and ask the children if they have seen animals in books or on television chasing or catching food to eat. Ask them to describe what happened.
- Turn to page 10 and discuss in what ways the fish and spider are clever. (*by hiding, pretending to be a rock; by spinning a web*) Ask: Which animal in the book do you think is the most skilled in how it gets its food? Why?
- Turn to pages 22 and 23. Ask the children to describe the trick that each creature uses to get its food, referring back if necessary.